LIKE
MOTHER
LIKE
Daughter

from our home to yours

**Randi Cola &
Michelle Cola Hasen**

Photography / Prop Styling
ARIEL TARR

Food Styling
MICHELLE DIAMOND

Additional Photography
MICHELLE LITTLE & AUTUMN WOOD

For my mom,
my best friend and my greatest inspiration
in the kitchen and in life

Recipes celebrating a mother-daughter bond in and outside of the kitchen

Ever since I was a little girl, I always loved standing by my mother's side as she prepared the most beautiful and delicious meals for our family and friends. As I grew up, my mom encouraged me to help in the kitchen and I always looked forward to doing so, because it meant spending time with my mom. We've always shared a close relationship. My mom was not only someone I went to for advice, she was also and still is, my best friend. My mom is someone I enjoy spending time with, and that time is more often than not time spent together in the kitchen.

My mom and I could sit down for lunch on a Tuesday and after only two sips of coffee, she will start reciting her menu for Shabbat dinner. I will then remind her that it's only Tuesday but she will quickly respond how she needs to order meat on Thursday, which is a mere two days away. We laugh as we go on to discuss the menu as if we're planning Rosh Hashanah dinner for thirty people (which, by the way, is pretty much the same conversation).

If you know my mother, you know how talented and creative she is. Our entire family and all of our friends love my mother's cooking and baking. Friends will seek out invitations to our house just to indulge in one of her home-cooked meals! I learned that no meal was too big or too small and that a simple week night meal was just as thrilling as preparing weekly Shabbat dinners, high holiday meals, Mother's Day brunches, Father's Day barbeques, birthday dinners, etc.

When I was engaged, my mother presented me with the greatest gift: a cookbook she compiled.

"FROM OUR HOME TO YOURS: TO MY MAYDEE WITH LOVE."

From generation to generation, food has always been and will always continue to be at the centre of so many happy times together as a family. Not only is it a proud reflection of our Jewish heritage, it is also a symbol of my love for you. Whether it's a birthday or anniversary, a Shabbat dinner, a Yom Tov, a welcome home, a Bon Voyage, A Mother's Day Brunch, a Father's Day Barbeque or a simple comfy weekday dinner, it ultimately became and continues to be special to plan it, serve it and share it with my biggest blessings in life; daddy, you and your brothers. My precious maydeleh, you now have a new beginning of your own. I cherish our culinary adventures together; so many of which shaped who I am today, both in and out of the kitchen! I look forward to sharing in your gastronomic ventures and I know I will learn new things along the way! May G-d bless you with a warm and loving home and may you always derive a sense of gratitude and pleasure in cooking for those you love.

Love, Mom

The recipes from the cookbook she presented to me make up most of this book; dishes that when I eat them I can close my eyes and imagine being a little girl again and recipes that when I simply smell them baking in the oven I can remember sharing with people who are no longer physically with us today. Food really does touch our souls.

This cookbook, "Like Mother, Like Daughter" starts off with our favourite appetizers, soups, salads and salad dressings, sides, fish, meat and poultry and of course an extensive dessert and baked goods section. A specific "Sunday brunch" is included since it has always been a favourite meal. The "Jewish Tradition" chapter contains recipes from grandparents or great-grandparents and typical recipes for specific Jewish holidays, which can of course be enjoyed at any time of year.

I dedicate my efforts of this cookbook to my mom as an ode to her unconditional love, support, strength and determination in all that she does. One of the greatest compliments I receive is when someone tells me that I am like my mother.

Mom, thank you for instilling in me a love of cooking and baking. Now that I am blessed as the mother of three beautiful children, Benjamin, Frankie and Isadora, I look forward to having them stand by me in the kitchen and hope that I can instil in them a love for cooking and baking as you did me.

"A daughter is the happy memories of the past, the joyful moments of the present and the hope and promise of the future"

Table of contents

There's always
time for a
Cocktail

Michelle Little & Autumn Wood

Starters

Randi's Guacamole

2	ripe avocados
1 tablespoon	fresh lime or lemon juice
2 tablespoons	red onion, minced or
	green onion, thinly sliced
1 to 2	serrano chilis, stems & seeds
	removed, minced
2 tablespoons	fresh cilantro, finely chopped
	salt & pepper, to taste
½	ripe tomato, seeds & pulp
	removed, chopped

Cut avocados in half, remove seed, score inside of avocado with blunt knife and scoop out flesh with a spoon. Place in a bowl. Using a fork, roughly mash the avocado. Don't overdo it, the guacamole should be a little chunky. Sprinkle with salt and lime (or lemon) juice.

Add chopped onion, chilis, cilantro, salt, pepper, and tomatoes. Start with half of one chili pepper and add to guacamole desired degree of hotness. Cover with plastic and chill until ready to serve.

Yields: 4 servings

Seasonal **Bruschetta**

4	ripe tomatoes, diced
3 or 4	shallots, diced
⅓ cup	fresh basil leaves, julienned & more for garnish
2 or 3	garlic cloves, minced
½ teaspoon	salt
¼ teaspoon	freshly ground pepper
1	baguette
3 tablespoons	olive oil
1	garlic clove, whole

In a medium bowl, combine tomatoes, shallots, basil, garlic, salt, pepper and 1 tablespoon olive oil.

Drizzle remaining olive oil over baguette slices and grill. Rub grilled baguette with whole garlic clove and spoon tomato mixture on top of baguette slices.

Garnish with basil right before serving.

Yields: 4 servings

Smoked *Whitefish* Dip

½ cup	mayonnaise
½ cup	sour cream
1 tablespoon	prepared horseradish
1 tablespoon	worcestershire sauce
2 tablespoons	dijon mustard
1 teaspoon	smoked paprika .
2	fresh lemons, zest & juice
2 tablespoons	tabasco sauce (optional)
1 teaspoon	cayenne powder
3	green onions, thinly sliced
1	celery stalk, finely diced
½	jalapeño, finely chopped (optional)
½	medium yellow onion, finely diced
1 pound	smoked whitefish, skinned & flaked
	salt & pepper, to taste
1 tablespoon	chives, finely chopped, for garnish

Prepare dressing by mixing mayonnaise, sour cream, horseradish, worcestershire, mustard, paprika, lemon zest and juice, hot sauce (if desired), cayenne, green onions, celery, jalapeño (if desired) and onion in medium bowl.

Season with salt and pepper to taste.

Place skinned and flaked whitefish in larger bowl. Pour dressing over fish.

Garnish with chives and serve with crackers. Any remaining sauce can be used with any other smoked fish. Sauce can keep in fridge up to 3-4 days.

Yields: 6 servings

Hot Artichoke Dip

1-8 ounce	block cream cheese, at room temperature
2 cups	mayonnaise
14 ounces	canned artichoke hearts, drained & chopped
2	green onions, thinly sliced
½ cup	grated fresh parmesan
1 cup	shredded mozzarella
dash	hot sauce
dash	worcestershire sauce
	salt & pepper, to taste

Preheat oven to 350°F.

In large mixing bowl, beat cream cheese with handheld electric mixer until smooth, then beat in mayonnaise until smooth. Add remaining ingredients and stir together until combined.

Transfer dip to pie plate or shallow gratin dish. Bake in oven 30-40 minutes until top is golden brown and dip is bubbling.

Serve hot with crackers, tortilla chips, crostini or veggies.

Yields: 6-8 servings

Spring  Rolls

Aromatics

2 tablespoons	fresh ginger, peeled & chopped
1 tablespoon	garlic, chopped
2 tablespoons	green onions, chopped
pinch	red pepper flakes
½ cup	peanut oil
pinch	salt & pepper
pinch	sugar

Filling

½ cup	sweet onions, julienned
1	carrot, julienned
4 ounces	shiitake mushrooms, stems discarded, julienned
1 ½ cups	red bell peppers, julienned
2 cups	green cabbage, julienned
3 tablespoons	peanut oil, for stir-frying
	salt & pepper
4 ounces	glass noodles, soaked in water for 10 minutes & chopped into small strands
¼ cup	soy sauce
2 tablespoons	chili paste
1 tablespoon	sesame oil
½ cup	cilantro, chopped

Spring Rolls

1 package	spring roll wrappers
	peanut oil, for deep-frying
	plum sauce, for dipping

To prepare aromatic mixture: in food processor, combine ginger, garlic, green onions and red pepper flakes. Turn on machine, slowly add oil and process mixture to purée. Cook mixture in small saucepan over medium heat 1-2 minutes. Season with salt, pepper and sugar. Set aside.

To prepare filling: in wok or heavy skillet, stir-fry mushrooms in peanut oil for 30 seconds, then add remaining vegetables and cook for 1 minute. Season with salt and pepper. Drain and transfer to a mixing bowl. Stir in noodles, mushroom soy sauce, chili paste, sesame oil and cilantro. Add aromatics mixture. Season with salt and pepper. Set aside to cool completely. When ready to form the spring rolls, squeeze out all the excess liquid.

To make spring rolls: place about ¼ cup of prepared filling per spring roll wrapper at about ¼ of way to the middle. Roll the wrapper, tuck ends in, and complete as if wrapping a parcel. Seal edges with a mixture of 1 tablespoon of both water and cornstarch, beaten together to use as egg wash. Repeat process until all filling is used.

In heavy deep saucepan, heat oil to 350°F and deep-fry spring rolls, 3 or 4 at a time until golden, about 2 to 3 minutes. Drain on paper towels.

Serve with store-bought plum sauce for dipping.

Yields: 24 rolls

Duck **Wontons** with Sweet Soy Sauce

Filling

4	whole duck legs, roasted
	salt & pepper
2	scallions, finely sliced
2 teaspoons	red onion, minced

Sauce

½ cup	soy sauce
½ cup	sugar
1 teaspoon	fresh ginger, minced
1	garlic clove, minced
1 teaspoon	Jack Daniels whiskey

Wontons

36	6"x 6" eggroll wrappers
	peanut oil, for frying

Preheat oven to 325°F .

Butterfly duck and season generously with salt and pepper. Roast uncovered 2 to 2½ hours. Baste occassionally with juices from duck, until cooked.

To prepare sauce, add all ingredients to small pot and cook on low medium heat until sugar has dissolved and sauce thickens slightly. Store in airtight container until ready to serve.

Let duck cool and then cut meat off duck bones. Using very sharp knife or food processor, chop duck meat up very well. Place into bowl and add scallions and red onion. Mix well. Add 3 teaspoons of sweet soy sauce mixture.

To assemble, lay the eggroll wrappers flat. Rub some duck fat from skin of roasted duck or egg wash around edge of each wrapper to moisten it. Place small amount of filling in centre. Make a purse by pleating and gathering ends of the dough as you enclose the filling. Preheat peanut oil and deep fry wontons in hot oil for 3-4 minutes. Remove to drain on paper towel.

Serve dipping sauce alongside wontons.

Wontons can be made earlier in the day. Leave at room temperature and warm right before serving in oven at 400°F for 5-7 minutes, until crispy.

Yields: 36 wontons

Jalapeño
Salmon
Tartare

1 pound	salmon, skinless & boneless
2	jalapeño peppers, finely diced
1	small sweet onion, finely sliced
1 tablespoon	olive oil
	kosher salt
	salt & pepper, to taste
2 tablespoons	fresh dill, chopped

Cut salmon into matchstick pieces ⅛" x ½" and place in airtight container covering generously with kosher salt. Leave fish to salt **overnight**.

In the **morning**, gently rinse salmon with cold water and pat dry with paper towels until all water is absorbed.

Add finely diced jalapeños, finely sliced vidalia onion, olive oil, salt, pepper and dill to taste.

Store in airtight container up to 1 week.

Yields: 8 servings

Classic Ceviche

1 pound	fresh, skinless snapper, bass, or halibut, cut into ½" cubes
1 ½ cups	fresh lime juice
1	medium white onion, chopped into ½" pieces
2	fresh tomatoes (about 1 pound) chopped into ½" pieces
1	avocado
1	jalapeño, stemmed, seeded & diced
⅓ cup	fresh cilantro, chopped
⅓ cup	green olives, pitted & chopped (optional)
2 tablespoons	fresh orange juice
½ teaspoon	salt

In 1 ½ quart glass or stainless steel bowl, combine fish, lime juice and onion. Use enough juice to cover fish and allow to float freely; too little juice means unevenly "cooked" fish.

Cover and refrigerate for about **4 hours**, until cube of fish no longer looks raw when broken open. Drain in a colander.

In large bowl, mix together tomatoes, jalapeño, cilantro and olives. Stir in fish and season with salt. Add the orange juice.

Cover and refrigerate if not serving immediately. Just before serving, gently stir in the diced avocado.

Yields: 8 servings

Crab Cakes
with Red Pepper Sauce

Crab Cakes

1	extra-large egg
3 tablespoons	mayonnaise
4 teaspoons	dijon mustard
1 tablespoon	fresh lemon juice
1 pound	mock crab, finely shredded
1 cup	white breadcrumbs or panko
½ cup	green onions, chopped
2 tablespoons	fresh parsley, chopped
1 teaspoon	salt
½ teaspoon	pepper
dash	cayenne pepper
	egg and panko crumbs, for coating
	vegetable or canola oil, for frying

Sauce

7 ounces	jarred roasted red peppers, drained
1 cup	mayonnaise
2 tablespoons	fresh parsley
2 large	garlic cloves
1 teaspoon	dijon mustard
½ teaspoon	fresh lemon juice
2 tablespoons	fresh parsley

Whisk first 4 crab cake ingredients in large bowl to blend. Add crab, breadcrumbs, green onions, parsley, salt and pepper. Combine well.

Form 1 generous tablespoon of mixture into ball: flatten and dip in egg and then panko crumbs. Pack well and let sit in refrigerator until ready to fry. Cakes keep shape better when refrigerated for a few hours.

Heat oil in skillet and cook crab cakes in batches on each side until brown, adding oil as necessary.

Combine ingredients for sauce, mixing well in a blender. Serve alongside crab cakes.

Crab cakes freeze well. Sauce lasts 3-4 days in airtight container in fridge.

Yields: 16 large or 24 small crabcakes

Lettuce **Wraps**
with
Hoisin Chicken

Sauce

4 tablespoons	hoisin sauce
2 tablespoons	rice vinegar
4 teaspoons	garlic, minced
1½ teaspoons	fresh ginger, minced
1 teaspoon	sesame oil

Filling

12 ounces	lean ground chicken or beef
1 teaspoon	vegetable oil
⅓ cup	carrots, finely diced
¾ cup	red peppers, finely diced
¾ cup	mushrooms, chopped
½ cup	canned water chestnuts, chopped
3	green onions, chopped

Lettuce Wraps

4 tablespoons	hoisin sauce
2 tablespoons	water
1	head iceberg or boston lettuce

To prepare sauce, whisk together hoisin, vinegar, garlic, ginger and sesame oil in a small bowl. Set aside.

To prepare chicken or beef, cook in skillet in small amount of oil. Drain and set aside. In same skillet, add a little more oil and cook vegetables until softened. Return beef or chicken to skillet with water chestnuts and green onions. Add sauce and cook for 2 minutes.

Divide filling among lettuce leaves. Serve open faced or rolled up.

Mix hoisin sauce and water in small bowl. Drizzle on top.

Yields: 4-6 servings

Soups, **Salads**  *Dressings*

Chicken **Soup**

6 quarts	water
1 ½	chickens, cut up
1	turkey drumstick (optional)
2 pounds	carrots, cut to 6" pieces
6	celery stalks
1 pound	bag parsnips
1	large (2 small) celery roots, peeled & cut in ½
4	leeks, cut in ½
1	bunch fresh dill
	salt, to taste

Bring water to boil. Lower temperature and add chicken. Return to boil and begin "skimming" the top so a clean pot of water remains. Add all vegetables and salt. Cook on low heat, uncovered for about 2-3 hours. Do not let boil. Turn off the heat and leave covered until ready to serve. Before ready to serve you may strain soup reserving the chicken on the side. Discard all vegetables except for carrots and parsnips. Adjust seasoning to taste. Garnish with the fresh dill.

Served best with egg noodles and homemade matzah balls (see page 165). Freezes well without carrots or parsnips for 3-4 months.

Yields: 12 servings

Cabbage Soup

1 ½ to 2 pounds	meaty flanken, bone-in strips
4 to 6 cups	green cabbage, shredded (or 2 bags pre-shredded cabbage)
1	large sweet onion, peeled & thinly sliced
2 tablespoons	vegetable or canola oil
12 cups	(2-48 ounce) tomato juice
1	lemon, juiced
½ to ¾ cup	sugar
	salt & pepper, to taste

In a large pot, place meat in enough water to cover. Bring to boil and skim the top as it cooks. Reduce heat to low and cook until tender. Remove meat and set aside.

In a large stock pot, heat oil and sauté onion until golden. Add cabbage, meat and remaining ingredients, except brown sugar. Stir on medium heat until combined well. Slowly add sugar to taste. Cook for 1 ½-2 hours. Adjust heat to simmer if begins to boil. When meat is fork tender remove from heat.

Recipe can easily be doubled for a larger crowd. Freezes very well.

Yields: 8 servings

Mushroom Barley Soup

2 tablespoons	canola or olive oil
2	large sweet onions, peeled & chopped
3	celery stalks, trimmed & chopped
3	garlic cloves, minced
8 cups	hot chicken or vegetable broth
3	potatoes, peeled or unpeeled, cut into small cubes
3	carrots, peeled & chopped
2 cups	mushrooms, trimmed & sliced
½ cup	pearl barley
	pepper
½ teaspoon	dried thyme
1 teaspoon	dried basil
1 or 2	turkey or chicken legs (optional: adds more flavour)
2 teaspoons	salt
2 tablespoons	fresh parsley
¼ cup	fresh dill

Sauté onions and celery in hot oil. Stir in garlic and sauté 2 to 3 minutes longer.

Add remaining ingredients except salt, parsley and dill. Bring to a boil. Stir gently and reduce heat.

Cover partially and simmer for about an hour, stirring occasionally until barley is tender.

If soup is too thick, add a little hot water. Add salt, parsley and dill.

Yields: 8-10 servings

Squash Soup

¾ pound	butternut squash
1 ¾ pounds	acorn squash
6 tablespoons	(¾ stick) unsalted butter or margarine
½ cup	white onion, peeled, trimmed and finely diced
4 cups	chicken or vegetable stock
½ teaspoon	salt
⅛ teaspoon	white pepper
¼ teaspoon	ground nutmeg
¼ teaspoon	ground ginger
½ teaspoon	ground cinnamon
1 teaspoon	brown sugar
½	fresh lemon, juiced
1 cup	heavy cream (or non-dairy creamer)
1	sprig fresh rosemary

Preheat oven to 350°F.

Cut each squash in half and discard seeds. Brush cut sides with 2 tablespoons of melted butter or margarine. Season with salt, pepper and nutmeg. Arrange squash cut side down on baking sheet. Bake until tender, about 1 ½ hours. Cool, scoop out insides of the squash, and purée the flesh in a food processor. Reserve.

In medium stockpot, melt remaining 4 tablespoons of butter or margarine over medium heat. Add onion and cook, stirring, until onion has softened and is transluscent but not browned. Add puréed squash. Add the chicken stock, salt, pepper, ginger, cinnamon, brown sugar and lemon juice and stir until well combine. Bring to a light boil over medium-high heat, stirring occasionally, then reduce heat to medium-low and allow to simmer, uncovered for 20 to 30 minutes to blend flavours.

In small saucepan, heat cream with the rosemary sprig. Remove rosemary and pour cream into the soup. Transfer to blender, food processor or use immersion blender and process, in batches, for 2 or 3 minutes. Adjust seasoning to taste.

Yields: 8 servings

Strawberry Mango & Mixed Greens Salad

Dressing

½ cup	honey
¾ cup	olive oil
⅓ cup	balsamic vinegar
1 teaspoon	salt

Salad

8 cups	mixed greens
2 cups	dried cranberries
1 cup	strawberries, sliced
1	mango, peeled, pitted & cubed
½ cup	red onion, thinly sliced
1 cup	slivered almonds or pine nuts, toasted

Combine honey, oil, vinegar and salt in jar. Cover tightly and shake vigorously.

Combine greens, cranberries, strawberries, mango and onion in a large bowl, tossing well.

To serve, toss with enough dressing to coat. Sprinkle with almonds or pine nuts.

Yields: 4-6 servings

Hazelnut-Crusted *Goat Cheese* **Salad**

Goat Cheese

¼ cup	all-purpose flour
¼ cup	plain dry breadcrumbs
5 ounces	soft fresh goat cheese, cut into equal rounds, chilled
1	extra-large egg, beaten to blend
3 tablespoons	hazelnuts, coarsely chopped

Dressing

1 tablespoon	red wine vinegar
1 tablespoon	orange zest, grated
1 tablespoon	fresh orange juice
2 teaspoons	honey
¼ cup	olive oil
	salt & pepper, to taste

Salad

1	large bunch watercress, stems trimmed
1	large head Belgian endive, thinly sliced lengthwise

Preheat oven to 400°F.

Place flour and breadcrumbs on separate plates. Coat cheese rounds with flour. Dip cheese into egg, then into breadcrumbs, coating completely. Place on small baking sheet. Spoon hazelnuts on top of cheese. Gently press hazelnuts into cheese to adhere. Cover and refrigerate at least **30 minutes or overnight**.

Whisk vinegar, orange zest, orange juice and honey in medium bowl to blend. Gradually whisk in oil. Season with salt and pepper. Vinaigrette can be made 4 hours ahead. Store at room temperature; whisk before using.

Bake cheese until heated through and coated brown, about 10 minutes.

Toss watercress and endive in large bowl with enough vinaigrette to coat. Season greens with salt and pepper. Divide greens among 4 plates. Top with warm goat cheese rounds.

Variation

Panko-Crusted Goat Cheese Rounds: Follow directions for hazelnut crusted goat cheese rounds substituting hazelnuts for panko. Coat cheese rounds with flour; dip in egg and coat in panko crumbs gently pressing to adhere.

Yields: 4 servings

Crunchy
Oriental Salad

Salad

1	large nappa cabbage, coarsley shredded
½ cup	shallots, thinly sliced into rounds
8 ounces	canned water chestnuts, sliced
¼ cup	almonds, toasted
¼ cup	pine nuts, toasted
1 cup	crunchy soup style noodles

Dressing

¼ cup	rice vinegar
⅓ cup	canola or peanut oil
1 tablespoon	soy sauce
1 teaspoon	sesame oil
1 to 2 teaspoons	sugar

Combine shredded cabbage, shallots, water chestnuts and almonds in a large bowl. Set aside.

In a separate bowl, whisk together all the ingredients for the dressing and refrigerate until ready to serve.

Just before serving, pour dressing over salad and gently combine.

Scatter cabbage noodles over top and serve immediately.

Yields: 4-6 servings

Purple Cabbage

Mandarin and **Pine Nut** Salad

Salad

2 cups	red cabbage, shredded
1 cup	carrot, coarsley shredded
⅓ cup	pine nuts, toasted
11 ounces	canned mandarin oranges, drained (reserve 1 tablespoon of juice for dressing)
1 to 2	handfuls dried cranberries

Dressing

½ cup	olive oil
1 tablespoon	white or red wine vinegar
4 tablespoons	brown sugar
1 teaspoon	vegetable consommé powder
1 tablespoon	reserved juice from mandarins

Combine salad ingredients together in large bowl.

Whisk dressing ingredients together and refrigerate until ready to use.

Toss at least **1 hour before serving** to allow the flavours to blend.

Keeps well in refrigerator for 2-3 days.

Yields: 4-6 servings

Deconstructed *California* **Roll** Salad

Rice Salad

3 cups	sushi rice, brown rice or white rice, cooked
¼ cup	seasoned rice vinegar
1 tablespoon	sugar
1 teaspoon	salt
1 ¼ teaspoons	wasabi paste
1 ½ teaspoons	vegetable oil
1	carrot, julienned
½	large cucumber, peeled, halved lengthwise, cored & chopped
3	scallions, thinly sliced diagonally
3 tablespoons	Japanese pickled ginger, drained, sliced & coarsely chopped
1 tablespoon	sesame seeds, toasted
1	avocado
1 (6")	square toasted nori, cut into very thin strips with scissors

Dressing

2 teaspoons	wasabi powder
1 tablespoon	hot water
2 tablespoons	cold water
2 tablespoons	soy sauce
2 teaspoons	ginger juice (squeezed from freshly grated ginger root)

Bring vinegar, sugar and salt to a boil in very small saucepan, stirring constantly until sugar is dissolved, then cool 2 minutes. Transfer cooked rice to large bowl and stir in cooled vinegar mixture.

Whisk together wasabi, 1 ½ tablespoons water and oil in a bowl, then add rice, carrot, cucumber, scallions, pickled ginger, and sesame seeds. Toss gently.

Cut avocado in half, pit, peel and cut crosswise into ¼" thick slices.

To make dressing, stir wasabi powder into hot water then stir in cold water, soy sauce and ginger juice.

Serve salad sprinkled with nori strips and avocado. Drizzle with dressing over salad.

Keeps well in refrigerator without nori strips, avocado and dressing, which should be added only right before serving.

Yields: 8-10 servings

Bistro
Vinaigrette

Green Goddess
Dressing

Steakhouse
Vinaigrette

Flax Oil Dressing

Sweet & Sour
Vinaigrette

Bistro
Vinaigrette

3 tablespoons	balsamic vinegar
1 tablespoon	sherry or red wine vinegar
1 tablespoon	dijon mustard
1	small shallot, minced
½ teaspoon	fresh thyme leaves, minced
½ cup	olive oil
⅓ cup	walnut oil
	salt & pepper, to taste

In medium bowl, whisk together balsamic and sherry or red wine vinegar, dijon mustard, shallot and thyme. Slowly whisk in oils and when emulsified, season with salt and pepper. Refrigerate in a covered container. When ready to use, whisk again.

Delicious on a variety of salads, from your basic iceberg lettuce salad to a flavourful blend of mixed greens and herbs with cherry tomatoes.

Yields: 1 ½ cups

Steakhouse
Vinaigrette

¼ cup	sweet onion or scallion, chopped
3 tablespoons	fresh parsley, minced
2 tablespoons	pimento, chopped
1 ½ teaspoons	sugar
1 teaspoon	salt
½ teaspoon	cayenne pepper
½ teaspoon	drained capers (optional)
⅓ cup	wine or cider vinegar
¾ cup	olive oil

Whisk together all the ingredients. Store in refrigerator up to a week.

Delicious served along side iceberg wedge or romaine hearts.

Yields: 1 ½ cups

Sweet & Sour
Vinaigrette

2	garlic cloves, chopped
¼ cup	sugar
1 teaspoon	dry mustard
½ cup	apple cider vinegar
½ teaspoon	paprika
1 cup	olive oil
½ cup	ketchup

Chop garlic in blender and add remaining ingredients. Refrigerate until ready to use.

Delicious over baby spinach or any combination of greens. Top with mandarins, strawberries, cashews or almonds for perfect combination.

Yields: 2 cups

Healthy Flax Oil
Dressing

½ cup	flax oil
¼ cup	apple cider vinegar
2 tablespoons	tamari
1 teaspoon	dijon mustard
3	garlic cloves, minced
⅓ cup	honey

Blend well and refrigerate until ready to use.

Serve over your favourite greens, radicchio, endive or any combination of vegetables.

Yields: 1 cup

Green Goddess
Dressing

2	garlic cloves
4	green onions
¼ cup	parsley
4 to 5	anchovy fillets
½ cup	sour cream
1 cup	mayonnaise
2 tablespoons	wine vinegar
1 tablespoon	lemon juice

Blend all ingredients well in a food processor until smooth. Keep refrigerated until ready to serve, up to 2 days.

Yields: 1 ½ cups

Spiced  Pecans

¼ cup	butter or margarine
½ cup	brown sugar
¼ cup	water
1 teaspoon	salt
½ teaspoon	cayenne pepper
4 cups	pecans, halved

Preheat oven to 350°F.

Line baking sheet with parchment. Melt butter or margarine in skillet over medium heat. Add brown sugar, water, salt and cayenne pepper. Stir until sugar dissolves. Add nuts to mixture and cook until syrupy, stirring frequently, about 5 minutes. Transfer nuts to prepared baking sheet, spread out in single layer. Bake until golden; about 10 minutes.

Cool and store in airtight container 1-2 weeks.

Yields: 16 servings

Grilled *Salmon* with Tangy Salsa

Salmon

4	6 ounce salmon fillets, skinned
	vegetable or canola oil, for grill
	kosher salt & pepper

Salsa

2	large oranges, cut in segments
¼ cup	olive oil
¼ cup	fresh lemon juice
½ cup	fresh flat-leaf parsley, chopped
2	scallions, finely sliced
3 tablespoons	fresh mint leaves, chopped
2 tablespoons	capers, rinsed & drained
2 tablespoons	orange zest
1 teaspoon	lemon zest
1 teaspoon	crushed red pepper flakes
	salt & pepper, to taste

For salsa, add orange segments to a medium bowl. Add olive oil, lemon juice, parsley, scallions, mint, capers, orange zest, lemon zest, and red pepper flakes. Toss lightly and season with salt and pepper to taste. Set aside.

For the salmon, put a grill pan over medium-high heat or preheat gas or charcoal grill. Brush grilling rack with vegetable oil to keep salmon from sticking. Season salmon with salt and pepper to taste. Grill until fish flakes easily and is cooked through, about 3 to 4 minutes each side.

Transfer the salmon to platter and allow to rest 5 minutes. Spoon salsa on top of salmon or serve on the side.

Yields: 4 servings

Pistachio Lime Baked **Salmon**

6	6 ounce salmon fillets, with skin
1 cup	pistachio nuts, shelled & chopped
½ cup	dark brown sugar
3 tablespoons	fresh lime juice
1 ½ teaspoons	fresh dill, chopped
1 ½ teaspoons	pepper
	kosher salt

Preheat oven to 425°F.

Place salmon in a 9" x 13" sprayed baking dish. Pat salmon with paper towel to remove excess water.

Combine ingredients in a small bowl. Spoon over salmon and bake for 12-15 minutes. Don't overcook the salmon. Remove from oven and serve hot or at room temperature.

Yields: 6 servings

Black Sea Bass
with Fresh Tomato &

Sea Bass

4	6 to 8 ounces black sea bass fillets with skin, any bones removed
2 tablespoons	olive oil
½ medium	red onion, thinly sliced
6	oregano sprigs
	salt & pepper, to taste

Salad

1	garlic clove
½ teaspoon	anchovy paste
2 tablespoons	red wine vinegar
¼ cup	olive oil
½ pound	grape tomatoes (preferably mixed colours), halved
½ pound	cherry tomatoes (preferably mixed colours), quartered
12	kalamata olives, pitted & halved or whole
4	sundried tomatoes packed in oil, chopped
1½ tablespoons	fresh oregano, chopped

Preheat oven to 425°F.

To make salad, mince and mash garlic to form paste with ½ teaspoon salt. Transfer to bowl and whisk in anchovy paste, vinegar and ¼ teaspoon pepper. Whisk in oil. Toss with remaining salad ingredients.

Add oil to a 1 ½ to 2 quart shallow baking dish. Rub flesh sides of fish with 2 teaspoons oil and season with salt and pepper. Divide onion slices and oregano sprigs into 2 portions and sandwich each portion between 2 fillets, skin- side out. Tie with kitchen string crosswise at 2" intervals and transfer to baking dish. Score skin on top in several places with a sharp knife and drizzle with remaining 4 teaspoons oil.

Roast fish until just cooked through, about 15 minutes. Cut off string and cut sandwiched fillets in half crosswise. If desired, pan fry fish fillets on each side in olive oil until cooked through making a crispy skin. Serve topped with salad.

Salad can be made earlier in the day and kept at room temperature.

Yields: 4 servings

Salt Baked

Branzino

1	2 pound whole branzino (European sea bass) or small sea bass, cleaned; head & tail left intact
3 pounds	sea salt
6 large	egg whites
4	sprigs rosemary
6	fresh parsley sprigs
4	lemon slices
	olive oil

Preheat oven to 400°F.

In a large bowl, whisk together egg whites and salt to form a sand-like paste. Lay out a baking sheet to hold the fish. Cover sheet with ¼" layer of salt. Lay fish on salt. Stuff fish with rosemary, parsley and lemon. Pack remaining salt over top of fish until fish is sealed well. Bake until salt is golden, about 30 minutes.

To serve, crack open salt crust . Filet fish and drizzle with good olive oil. Season lightly with salt and pepper.

Yields: 2-3 servings

Whole-Fried **Snapper** with *Ginger Sauce*

Snapper

1	2 to 3 pound fresh snapper, cleaned and scaled, tail trimmed with head on
	flour, seasoned with salt, to taste
	vegetable oil, for frying

Sauce

1	large vidalia onion, julienned
1	red pepper, julienned
1 cup	shiitake mushrooms, julienned
6 tablespoons	rice vinegar
6 tablespoons	sugar
¾ cup	water
2 tablespoons	soy sauce
2 tablespoons	scallion, finely chopped
1 tablespoon	cornstarch
1 tablespoon	cold water
4 tablespoon	fresh ginger, peeled & julienned
1	sprig cilantro (optional)

To prepare ginger sauce, sauté onion, red pepper and mushrooms in saucepan until soft. Transfer small dish and reserve pan. Add vinegar, sugar, water and soy sauce to reserved saucepan and boil for 5 minutes. Add scallions, using most of the green portion as well. Blend cornstarch with cold water until smooth in small bowl, then stir into sauce. Cook, stirring until clear and thickened. Remove from heat. Stir in ginger and reserved vegetables. Keep warm until fish is ready.

Preheat oil in skillet, enough to cover bottom, on high heat until it reaches 350°F. Wash fish well and pat dry thoroughly with paper towels. With sharp knife slash fish diagonally on each side almost to centre bone. Dip fish in seasoned flour, then dust off excess flour. Deep fry in hot oil until golden brown, drain on absorbent paper, then transfer fish carefully to serving dish, spoon sauce and serve immediately. Garnish with a sprig of fresh cilantro, if desired.

Diced pineapple chunks can be added to sauce for a sweet tropical flavour.

Yields: 2 servings

Asian Style
Crispy
Black Bass

1	2 to 3 pound whole fresh black bass, cleaned & scaled, fins trimmed
8	thinly sliced fresh ginger, peeled
½ cup	sake
½ cup	low-sodium soy sauce
¼ cup	fresh lemon juice
1 teaspoon	sugar
2	scallions, thinly sliced
	peanut oil, for deep-frying
	salt & pepper
	cornstarch

Make 4 deep, diagonal slashes down to the bone on both sides of fish. Insert ginger into slashes. Refrigerate fish until ready to cook.

In small saucepan, bring sake, soy sauce, lemon juice, and sugar to a boil. Remove pan from the heat, and let it cool. Stir in sliced scallions.

Fill wok or deep-fryer, large enough to hold fish with peanut oil to cover fish by 1". Heat oil until very hot, about 375°F on deep-frying thermometer. Season fish lightly all over with salt and pepper, then dust lightly but evenly with cornstarch.

Hold fish by the tail, carefully slip it and away from you into hot oil head first. Fry until the skin is crispy and golden brown and the flesh is cooked through, flaky and separates easily from bone, about 10 minutes.

With long-handled metal tongs, remove fish from wok or fryer, letting excess oil drip back into wok. Transfer fish to serving platter. Serve immediately with excess sauce on the side.

Garnish fish with scallion strips, cilantro and squeeze lemon half over it.

Yields: 2 servings

Miso Glazed Cod

4	6 ounce black cod fillets, with skin
⅓ cup	sake
⅓ cup	mirin
⅓ cup	light yellow miso
3 tablespoons	brown sugar
2 tablespoons	soy sauce
	green onions, for garnish

Preheat oven to 400°F.

Prepare the marinade by bringing sake and mirin to a boil in a medium saucepan over high heat. Boil for 20 seconds to evaporate the alcohol. Turn heat down to low, add the miso paste, and whisk. When the miso has dissolved completely, turn the heat up to high again and add sugar and soy sauce, whisking constantly to ensure that sugar doesn't burn on the bottom of the pan. Remove from heat once sugar is fully dissolved. Cool to room temperature.

Pat the black cod fillets dry thoroughly with paper towels. Slather the fish with miso marinade and place in non-reactive dish or bowl and cover tightly with plastic wrap. **Leave to marinate in refrigerator for 2 to 3 days.**

Heat an ovenproof skillet over high heat on stovetop. Lightly wipe off any excess miso clinging to fillets, but don't rinse it off. Film pan with a little oil, then place fish skin-side-up on the pan and cook until bottom of fish browns and blackens in spots, about 3 minutes. Flip and continue cooking until other side is browned, 2 to 3 minutes. Transfer to oven and bake for 5 to 10 minutes until fish is opaque and flakes easily.

Garnish with green onions.

Yields: 4 servings

Poultry & Beef

Tuscan Chicken

1	whole chicken, butterflied & flattened
⅓ cup	olive oil
2 teaspoons	fresh lemon zest (from 2 lemons), grated
⅓ cup	freshly squeezed lemon juice
1 tablespoon	garlic, minced
1 tablespoon	fresh rosemary leaves, minced
	kosher salt & pepper
1	lemon, halved

Season chicken generously with salt. Combine olive oil, lemon zest, lemon juice, garlic, rosemary and 2 teaspoons pepper in a small measuring cup. Place the chicken in a ceramic or glass dish just large enough to hold it flat. Pour the lemon marinade over the chicken, turning it in the dish. Cover the dish with plastic wrap and refrigerate for at least **4 hours or overnight**. Turn the chicken 2 or 3 times while marinating.

Preheat grill to medium-high. When ready, place the chicken skin-side up, and weigh it down with the dish used for marinating.

Cook 12 to 15 minutes, until the underside is golden brown. Turn the chicken skin-side down, weight again with the dish, and cook for another 12 to 15 minutes until the skin is golden brown and chicken is cooked through.

Place the lemon halves on the cool side of the grill, cut side down for the last 10 minutes of cooking. Remove the chicken to a plate or cutting board, cover with aluminum foil and allow to rest for 5 minutes. Cut in quarters, sprinkle with salt and serve with the grilled lemon halves.

Yields: 4 servings

Beer Can Chicken

Chicken

1	whole chicken, washed & dried
	vegetable oil
1	12 ounce can beer

Rub

2 tablespoons	smoked paprika
2 tablespoons	salt
2 tablespoons	onion powder
1 tablespoon	cayenne pepper
1 tablespoon	ground cumin
2 teaspoons	dried thyme
2 teaspoons	dried oregano
2 teaspoons	black pepper
2 teaspoons	garlic powder

To prepare the rub, mix all the ingredients together in a small bowl.

For the chicken, preheat grill to medium-high heat. Rub the chicken and its cavity with the vegetable oil. Season the chicken with rub mixture, remembering to season the cavity. Pour out ¼ of the beer and sit the chicken on top of the beer can.

Place the chicken in the centre of the hot grill and cover. Cook the chicken for 1 to 1 ½ hours, or until an instant-read thermometer registers 165°F.

Once cooked, cover loosely with foil and let rest for 10 minutes, remove beer can and carve.

If a less charred chicken is desired, you can remove from grill and finish cooking in a 350°F oven until chicken is cooked through. You can store extra rub mixture in an airtight container for up to 6 months.

Yields: 4 servings

Chicken

Marbella

1	whole chicken, cut in quarters
1 cup	pitted prunes
½ cup	pitted green olives
½ cup	capers (with 3 teaspoons liquid)
¼ cup	dried oregano
½ cup	red wine vinegar
½ cup	olive oil
1	head garlic, minced
	kosher salt & pepper
1 cup	brown sugar
1 cup	white wine
½ cup	fresh parsley, chopped

Preheat oven to 350°F.

Combine prunes, olives, capers, caper liquid, oregano, vinegar, olive oil and garlic in large shallow ovenproof dish. Season with salt and pepper. Add chicken, tossing to coat. Cover and refrigerate **8 hours or overnight.**

Uncover chicken and sprinkle with brown sugar. Pour wine over chicken and bake 1 hour covered. Uncover chicken and bake 30 minutes or until golden brown. Broil for 5 minutes if prefer the skin lightly brown. Garnish with parsley.

Allowing chicken to marinate overnight is essential to really soak up all the flavours as well as producing a tender and juicy chicken.

Yields: 4 servings

Duck Confit

1   duck leg, per person
5-6   slices beef fry
       (if a smoky flavour is desired)
       coarse sea salt or kosher salt

Pat duck legs dry with paper towels. With a very pointy knife pierce the skin of the duck all over. Focus on the skin that covers fat. Avoid piercing the meat itself by pricking the skin at an angle over the drumstick and the centre of the thigh. Salt duck legs very well.

Place strips of beef fry along the bottom of roasting pan or grease the pan with melted duckfat. Place the duck legs skin-side up, close together but not overlapping in pan. Place in the oven and turn it to 300°F. **Do not preheat the oven**, the duck should cook as gently as possible. When the skin is starting to look crispy, after about 2 ½ to 3 hours, turn the heat to 375°F. Check after 15 minutes. Duck legs should be light golden brown.

Remove from the oven and let cool for 10-15 minutes before eating.

Yields: 1 duck leg per person

Roast **Duck** Breasts
with
Pomegranate
Chili Sauce

Duck

8	5 to 6 ounce boneless duck breast halves, skin & fat trimmed
	coarse kosher salt

Sauce

⅓ cup	sugar
½ cup	water
2 cups	pomegranate juice (such as Pom)
2 cups	low-sodium chicken broth
4	large dried chilis stemmed, seeded, torn into 1" long pieces
1 ½ teaspoons	adobo sauce (from canned chipotle chilis in adobo)
1 ½ teaspoons	balsamic vinegar
⅔ cup	cherry jam
	coarse kosher salt
	pepper
	fresh pomegranate seeds, for garnish

Preheat oven to 400°F.

To prepare sauce, stir sugar and ½ cup water in heavy large saucepan over medium heat until sugar dissolves. Increase heat, boil until syrup is deep amber colour, swirling pan occasionally, about 8 minutes. Add juice, broth and chilis. Boil until sauce is reduced to 1 ½ cups, about 25 minutes. Remove from heat and cool. Purée in tightly covered blender until smooth, about 2 minutes. Transfer to bowl. Whisk in adobo sauce, vinegar, and jam. Season to taste with generous amount of coarse salt and pepper.

Score skin of duck (don't cut into flesh) with 5 cuts in 1 direction; repeat in opposite direction, making diamond pattern. Sprinkle duck all over with coarse salt and pepper.

Place 2 large ovenproof skillets over medium-high heat. Add duck, skin-side down, to skillets, dividing equally. Cook duck until skin is crisp and deep brown, about 7 minutes. Turn duck over; cook 1 minute. Pour off fat. Transfer skillets to oven. Roast duck until cooked to medium-rare, about 5 minutes.

Transfer duck to cutting board. Let rest 5 minutes. Thinly slice each breast crosswise on slight diagonal. Arrange slices on plates. Spoon sauce over and sprinkle with pomegranate seeds.

Yields: 8 servings

Honey Soy *Ginger* Duck

Duck

2	ducks, cut into quarters
½ cup	onions, diced
¼ cup	fresh ginger, peeled & diced
½ cup	soy sauce
1 cup	water

Sauce

1 cup	honey
½ cup	plum sauce
¼ cup	soy sauce
2 tablespoons	fresh ginger, minced
1 teaspoon	flour mixed with 2 tablespoons of cold water

Preheat oven to 350°F.

To prepare duck, finely chop onions and ginger in food processor. Add soy sauce with 1 cup water and blend. Thoroughly coat duck and cover with plastic wrap and refrigerate for at least **6 hours or overnight**.

Remove duck from marinade, wiping off the excess and reserving the marinade. Place duck in a roasting pan and strain marinade over them. Bake for 1 hour or until duck is tender, basting every 15 minutes with juices in pan.

While duck is roasting, prepare honey ginger sauce and keep warm by combining all sauce ingredients except flour mixture and bring to a boil. Whisk in the flour-water mixture, reduce to low, and simmer until sauce is syrupy, about 20 minutes. Keep warm.

When duck is ready, drizzle sauce over duck pieces and serve with extra sauce on the side.

Yields: 8 servings

Rack of *Lamb* with Fresh Herbs & Garlic

3	1 to 1¼ pounds well-trimmed racks of lamb, 8 bones per pack
10	garlic cloves, peeled
½ cup	fresh mint leaves
¼ cup	fresh parsley leaves
¼ cup	fresh rosemary leaves
2 teaspoons	herbes de Provence
	kosher salt
2 teaspoons	coarsely ground black pepper
6 tablespoons	olive oil

Preheat oven to 450°F.

Combine garlic, herbs, salt and pepper in food processor and pulse until garlic is finely chopped. Add 4 tablespoons oil and blend until coarse paste forms. Sprinkle each lamb rack generously with kosher salt. Transfer half the herb paste to small bowl and reserve. Spread remaining half of herb paste over lamb racks. Arrange lamb on rimmed baking sheet. Let stand at room temperature **2 hours**.

Combine remaining 2 tablespoons oil in heavy large skillet over high heat. Place 1 lamb rack, meat side down, in skillet. Sear until golden, about 2 minutes; return to baking sheet, meat side up. Repeat with remaining lamb racks.

Roast lamb in oven until meat thermometer inserted into centre of lamb registers 130°F for medium-rare, about 20 minutes. Transfer lamb to platter. Let stand 15 minutes. Mix any pan juices into reserved herb paste. Cut lamb between bones into individual chops.

Can be made 1 day ahead: cover lamb and reserved herb paste separately and chill. Bring both to room temperature before continuing.

Yields: 6 servings

Lamb Chops with Dried Cherries & Port

4	lamb chops, double cut or 8 single cut
2 teaspoons	olive oil
⅓ cup	shallots, chopped
¾ cup	Port
½ cup	chicken broth
½ cup	dried tart cherries
3 tablespoons	cherry jam
1 teaspoon	balsamic vinegar
½ teaspoon	ground cardamom
	kosher salt & pepper
	fresh mint or parsley, for garnish

Heat oil in heavy medium non-stick skillet over medium-high heat. Sprinkle lamb with salt and pepper. Add lamb to skillet; cook to desired doneness, turning often, about 10 minutes for medium-rare. Transfer lamb to plate. Pour off drippings from skillet.

Add shallots to same skillet; sauté 1 minute. Add Port, broth, cherries, jam, vinegar, and cardamom; boil until cherries plump and liquid is syrupy, about 6 minutes. Season with salt and pepper. Spoon sauce over lamb.

Sprinkle with fresh mint or fresh parsley.

A full bodied sweet red wine, such as a Merlot or Chianti may be substituted for Port.

Yields: 2 servings

Roast Lamb
with
Berry-Pecan Crust

2	1 to 1 ½ pound racks of lamb, well trimmed
6 tablespoons	blackberry jam
¼ cup	dijon mustard
¾ cup	pecans, finely chopped
6 tablespoons	fresh Italian parsley, minced
¾ cup	fresh breadcrumbs
4 tablespoons	olive oil
	kosher salt & pepper

Preheat oven to 425°F.

Sprinkle lamb with salt and pepper. Combine jam and dijon mustard in small bowl; whisk to blend. Mix pecans, Italian parsley and fresh breadcrumbs in another small bowl to blend. Spread half of mustard glaze over the rounded side of each lamb rack. Pat half of the breadcrumb mixture over the mustard glaze on each. Drizzle each with 2 tablespoons of olive oil.

Transfer the lamb to large rimmed baking sheet. Roast until breadcrumb topping is golden; about 30 minutes. Cut racks between bones into individual chops and serve.

Yields: 6 servings

Michelle Little & Autumn Wood

Standing Rib **Roast**

1	12 to 13 pound prime rib roast, 5 ribs
⅓ cup	dijon mustard
2 tablespoons	garlic, minced
1 tablespoon	thyme leaves, chopped
2 teaspoons	coarsley ground pepper
	kosher salt
3 tablespoons	olive oil

Preheat oven to 450°F.

In small bowl, mix mustard with the garlic, thyme, pepper and 2 teaspoons of kosher salt. Whisk in olive oil.

Set the meat, bone side down, in a roasting pan and season lightly with salt. Roast the meat in the lower third of the oven for 20 minutes. Remove the meat from the oven and **reduce the temperature to 350°F**.

Brush the mustard coating all over top and sides of meat and roast for about 1 ½ hours longer, rotating roasting pan 2 or 3 times for even browning. Meat is done when instant-read thermometer inserted in centre of roast at the thickest part registers 120°F, for medium rare.

Transfer roast to carving board, cover loosely with foil and let rest for 20 to 30 minutes. Set roast on its side and run a long, sharp knife between the bones and meat; remove the bones and set them aside. Turn the roast right side up. Carve the roast ¼" to ½" thick and transfer slices to warmed plates. Pour any carving juices over the meat and serve.

A rich deep Burgundy wine is a classic pairing to this delicious Shabbat dinner or special celebration.

Yields: 10-12 servings

Horseradish
Crusted
Rib Roast

1	5 to 6 pound boneless rib roast
	salt & pepper
6 tablespoons	olive oil
6	garlic cloves, coarsely chopped
1 cup	prepared horseradish
3 tablespoons	fresh thyme
3 tablespoons	fresh rosemary
2 tablespoons	dijon mustard (more if needed for coating)

Preheat oven to 400°F.

Pat beef dry and sprinkle with salt and pepper. Brown beef on all sides in 3 tablespoons of olive oil in skillet until golden which will allow meat to retain its juices. Let rest until cool.

While meat cools, combine remaining 3 tablespoons olive oil, garlic, horseradish, thyme and rosemary in small bowl. Place meat in roasting pan and rub meat all over with mustard and then coat top and sides of meat with horseradish herb mixture, pressing well to adhere. Roast until meat is medium rare, about 15 minutes per pound.

Transfer to cutting board and cover for a few minutes before carving.

Yields: 4-6 servings

Slow-Cooker *Pulled* Barbecue **Beef**

1	3 pound boneless beef chuck roast
1½ cups	ketchup
¼ cup	brown sugar
¼ cup	barbecue sauce
2 tablespoons	worcestershire sauce
2 tablespoons	dijon mustard
1	teaspoon liquid smoke (optional)
½ teaspoon	salt
¼ teaspoon	garlic powder
¼ teaspoon	pepper
12	sandwich buns, split
	sliced pickles, for serving
	sliced onions, for serving
	sliced jalapeños, for serving

Cut roast in half and place in a 3 or 4 quart slow cooker. In small bowl, combine ketchup, brown sugar, barbecue sauce, worcestershire sauce, mustard, liquid smoke (if desired) and seasonings. Pour over beef. Cover and cook on low for **8 to 10 hours** or until meat is tender.

Remove meat; cool slightly. Skim fat from cooking liquid. Shred beef with two forks; return to the slow cooker. Cover and cook for 15 minutes or until heated through.

Using a slotted spoon, place ½ cup on each bun. Serve with sliced onions, pickles and jalapeños if desired.

Freezer option: place individual portions of cooled meat mixture in freezer containers. To use, partially thaw in refrigerator overnight. Microwave, covered, on high in a microwave-safe dish until heated through, gently stirring and adding a little broth / water if necessary.

Yields: 12 servings

Meaty *Spaghetti* Sauce

2 to 3 tablespoons	olive oil
2	onions, finely chopped
3	garlic cloves, finely chopped
1	red pepper, finely chopped
1 cup	mushrooms, sliced
2 pounds	ground beef
28 ounces	canned crushed tomatoes
11 ounces	canned tomato paste
¼ teaspoon	pepper
	salt, to taste
dash	cayenne pepper
1 teaspoon	sugar
1 teaspoon	dried oregano
1 teaspoon	dried basil
1	bay leaf
¼ cup	red wine

Sauté onions and garlic in olive oil in large saucepan on high heat until the onions are translucent, stirring regularly. Add red pepper and mushrooms, sauté until softened. Add ground beef and brown, stirring regularly until the beef is broken up.

Reduce heat to medium. Add tomatoes and tomato paste, stirring until well mixed. Add remaining seasonings, stirring frequently.

Reduce heat to low and let simmer for **2 to 3 hours**.

Serve with spaghetti or a pasta of your choice.

Yields: 8 servings

Barley Risotto

1 tablespoon	olive oil
1	large onion, chopped
1	red pepper, chopped
3	garlic cloves, minced
1½ cups	mushrooms, sliced
1½ cups	barley
3½ cups	chicken or vegetable broth
	salt & pepper, to taste
¼ cup	fresh dill, chopped

In large skillet, heat oil and sauté onion, red pepper, garlic and mushrooms until golden, 5 to 7 minutes. Stir in barley and cook until lightly toasted, about 5 minutes. Slowly stir in ½ cup hot broth. Cook, stirring until liquid evaporates. Stir in another ½ cup broth.

Repeat until you have added 2 cups of broth. Pour in remaining broth, cover and simmer for 45 minutes, until tender. If necessary, add a little water or broth to prevent sticking.

Add salt, pepper and dill.

Yields: 6-8 servings

Grilled Baby *Potatoes* with **Herbs**

3 pounds	small red-skinned potatoes
4 tablespoons	olive oil
1 cup	green onions, thinly sliced
3 tablespoons	Italian parsley, chopped
3	garlic cloves, finely chopped
2 teaspoons	fresh oregano, chopped
	salt & pepper, to taste
3 tablespoons	grated fresh parmesan, optional

Cook potatoes in large pot of boiling salted water until tender, about 15 minutes. Drain potatoes; cool.

Prepare barbecue on medium heat. Cut potatoes in half; transfer to large bowl. Add 2 tablespoons oil; toss to coat. Grill potatoes until golden, turning occasionally, about 5 minutes. Transfer to bowl. Drizzle 2 tablespoons oil over.

Add remaining ingredients; toss to coat. Season with salt and pepper. Serve warm.

Yields: 12 servings

Garlic **Roasted** Potato Skins

3 pounds	(6 to 8 large) baking potatoes
1	small head garlic
6 tablespoons	(¾ stick) unsalted butter or
	margarine, at room temperature
	salt & pepper, to taste

Preheat oven to 350°F.

Prick each potato once or twice with fork. Cut off and discard top fourth of garlic head, then wrap garlic tightly in foil. Bake garlic and potatoes on same rack in lower third of oven until potatoes are tender, approximately 1 hour. Remove potatoes and garlic from oven and cool on metal rack for 15 minutes.

Halve potatoes lengthwise, then quarter each half (to form short wedges). Scoop out almost all potato flesh (reserving it for another use, like mashed potatoes) leaving about ¼" thick layer of potato flesh inside each potato wedge.

Increase oven temperature to 425°F. Squeeze garlic into small bowl, discarding garlic skins, and mash to a paste with butter or margarine, salt and pepper using a fork. Divide garlic paste among potato skins (about ½ teaspoon each), spreading evenly, then roast skins in a large shallow baking pan (1"deep) until golden and crisp, 15-20 minutes.

For a heartier side dish, leave a thicker layer of potato.

Yields: 12 servings

Maple Roasted *Sweet* **Potatoes**

3	large sweet potatoes, peeled & cubed
12 ounces	frozen cranberries
½ cup	butter or margarine
½ cup	maple syrup
½ cup	pecans, chopped & toasted

Preheat oven to 375°F.

Place sweet potatoes and cranberries in large lightly greased roasting pan.

Combine butter and maple syrup. Pour over sweet potatoes and cranberries, stirring to coat. Cover tightly with foil.

Bake 30-35 minutes or until potatoes are tender. Spoon into a serving dish and sprinkle with pecans.

Yields: 12 servings

Sweet *Potato* Fritters

1 pound	red-skinned sweet potatoes (yams)
2 tablespoons	(¼ stick) butter, melted
⅓ cup	sugar
¾ tsp	salt
½ tsp	ground cinnamon
1	extra-large egg
1 cup	all-purpose flour
½ cup	fresh breadcrumbs made from crustless French bread
1 tablespoon	baking powder
	vegetable or canola oil, for frying
	maple syrup, for serving

Preheat oven to 350°F.

Pierce potatoes with fork and place directly on the rack in oven or on a baking sheet. Bake for approximately 45 minutes or until they feel soft inside when poked. When cool enough to handle, spoon enough cooked potato from skin into 1 cup measure to fill.

Transfer 1 cup potatoes to medium bowl; add butter and mash well. Mix in sugar, salt and cinnamon, then egg. Whisk flour, breadcrumbs and baking powder into potato mixture to make a dough.

Pour enough oil into heavy medium saucepan to reach depth of 1"; heat oil to 325°F. Working in batches, drop dough by heaping teaspoonfuls into oil. Fry until golden brown and cooked through, about 1 ½ minutes per side.

Using slotted spoon, transfer fritters to baking sheet; place in oven to keep warm. Repeat with remaining batter. Serve fritters hot with maple syrup.

Yields: 12 servings

Pecan **Noodle** Ring

1 cup	pecans, chopped
½ cup	brown sugar, packed
½ cup	butter or margarine, melted
16 ounces	broad egg noodles
6	extra-large eggs
1 cup	sugar
1 teaspoon	salt
1 teaspoon	ground cinnamon

Preheat oven to 350°F.

Combine pecans, brown sugar, and butter and spoon into fluted cake pan, bundt pan or two loaf pans.

Cook noodles according to package directions. Drain and transfer into a large bowl.

Add eggs, sugar, salt, and cinnamon, stirring well. Pour into prepared pan. Bake for 1 hour (less time will be needed if done in 2 loaf pans).

Remove from the oven and let cool. Turn out onto serving plate scraping up any pecans that may have stuck to the bottom.

Yields: 12 servings

Desserts

Baked Goods

Bittersweet
Chocolate
Soufflés

10 ounces	70% bittersweet chocolate, chopped
¼ cup	unsalted butter
5	extra-large eggs, separated
⅓ cup	sugar
1 tablespoons	unsweetened cocoa powder
1 ½ teaspoons	fresh lemon juice
	icing sugar, for dusting

Preheat oven to 375°F. Spray eight ramekins or custard cups with nonstick spray; coat ramekins or cups with 1 tablespoon sugar tapping out excess sugar.

Stir chopped chocolate and butter in large metal bowl set over saucepan of simmering water until mixtures is melted and smooth. Remove chocolate mixture from heat; cool slightly.

Using electric mixer, beat egg yolks, ⅓ cup sugar, and cocoa powder in medium bowl until thick ribbons of mixture form, about 3 minutes. Gently fold into chocolate mixture.

Using electric mixer with clean dry beaters, beat egg whites in medium bowl until foamy. Add lemon juice to beaten egg whites and beat until soft peaks form. Fold into chocolate mixture in 3 separate additions. Divide among prepared ramekins.

Bake soufflés until puffed above edges but still soft in centre, about 18 minutes. Bake chilled soufflés about 20 minutes. Dust the finished soufflé with icing sugar, if desired. Serve immediately.

Can be made 1 day ahead without baking. Cover and refrigerate. Bring to room temperature before baking.

Yields: 8 servings

Bubby Shirley's
Coffee Cake

Cinnamon Filling

1 cup	brown sugar
1 cup	walnuts, chopped
1 ½ teaspoons	ground cinnamon

Cake

2 cups	all-purpose flour
1 teaspoon	baking powder
1 teaspoon	baking soda
½ cup	(1 stick) unsalted butter, at room temperature
1 cup	sugar
3	extra-large eggs
1 cup	sour cream
1 ½ teaspoons	pure vanilla extract

Preheat oven to 350°F. Grease 10" tube pan; dust with flour, tapping out excess.

Mix brown sugar, walnuts and cinnamon in small bowl; set aside. Sift flour, baking powder and baking soda into medium bowl.

Using electric mixer, beat butter and sugar in large bowl until fluffy. Add eggs 1 at a time, beating just until combined after each addition. Mix in sour cream and vanilla. Add flour mixture and stir until blended. Spoon ½ of batter into prepared pan. Sprinkle ½ of cinnamon filling and then spoon remaining batter over. Sprinkle remaining cinnamon filling over top.

Bake cake until tester inserted near centre comes out clean, about 1 hour. Cool cake in pan 10 minutes. Cut around pan sides to loosen cake. Remove cake from pan, keeping it right-side up onto rack and cool completely.

Yields: 10-12 servings

Carrot Cake
with
Cream Cheese Frosting

Cake

2 cups	sugar
1 cup	vegetable oil
4	extra-large eggs
2 cups	all-purpose flour
2 teaspoons	baking powder
2 teaspoons	baking soda
1 teaspoon	salt
1 teaspoon	ground cinnamon
¾ teaspoon	ground nutmeg
3 cups	carrots, peeled & finely grated
½ cup	walnuts, chopped
1 cup	shredded coconut

Frosting

4 cups	icing sugar
2-8 ounce	cream cheese, at room temperature
½ cup	(1 stick) unsalted butter, at room temperature
4 teaspoons	pure vanilla extract

Preheat oven to 325°F. Lightly grease three 9" diameter cake pans with 1 ½" high sides. Line bottom of pans with parchment paper and lightly grease.

For cake, using electric mixer, beat sugar and vegetable oil in bowl until combined. Add eggs 1 at a time, beating well after each addition. Sift flour, baking powder, baking soda, salt, cinnamon and nutmeg into sugar and oil mixture. Stir in carrots, chopped walnuts and coconut.

Pour batter into prepared pans, dividing equally. Bake until toothpick inserted into centre comes out clean and cakes begin to pull away from sides of pans, about 45 minutes. Cool in pans on racks for 15 minutes. Turn out cakes onto racks and cool completely.

For frosting, using electric mixer beat all ingredients in medium bowl until smooth and creamy. Place 1 cake layer on platter. Spread with ¾ cup frosting. Top with another cake layer. Spread with ¾ cup frosting. Top with remaining cake layer. Using icing spatula, spread remaining frosting in decorative swirls over sides and top of cake.

Cake can be made 1 day ahead: wrap tightly in plastic and store at room temperature. If icing, place dome over cake and refrigerate. Garnish with shredded coconut and walnuts.

Yields: 12 servings

White Chocolate & Bittersweet
Chocolate Mousse Cake

Chocolate Mousse Cake
with Hazelnut Crust

Flourless Chocolate Cake
with Chocolate Ganache

Chocolate Mousse Cake with Hazelnut Crust

Hazelnut Crunch

5 ounces	hazelnut or praline flavoured chocolate, chopped
1 cup	Rice Krispies cereal
⅓ cup	hazelnuts, toasted & finely chopped

Cake

Any favourite rich and fudgy chocolate cake
(a devil's food cake or chocolate fudge cake mix works well)

Hazelnut Mousse

10 ounces	hazelnut or praline flavoured chocolate, chopped
1 ¼ cups	heavy whipping cream, chilled
⅛ teaspoon	salt
3 tablespoons	water
	cocoa powder, for dusting

To prepare hazelnut crunch, line bottom of 8" diameter spring form pan with parchment paper. Place praline or hazelnut chocolate in medium metal bowl; set bowl in hot water in skillet. Stir until melted and smooth. Stir in cereal and nuts. Spread crunch evenly over parchment in pan. Chill until crunch is firm, about 1 hour.

Prepare cake according to directions and cool in 8" pan. Place cooled cake on top of crunch pressing to adhere.

To prepare hazelnut mousse, place praline or hazelnut chocolate in medium metal bowl; set bowl in hot water in skillet. Stir until melted and smooth. Using electric mixer beat cream and salt in another bowl until very soft peaks form. Mix 3 tablespoons water into melted chocolate. Pour whipped cream over and fold into chocolate just until incorporated.

Spread mousse over cake in pan. Cover and chill **overnight.**

Run knife between cake and pan sides to loosen. Carefully remove pan sides from cake; smooth mousse with knife if necessary. Place cake on pan bottom on rack set over baking sheet. Sift cocoa powder lightly over top of cake. Transfer to platter and serve.

Can be prepared 2 days ahead and kept chilled.

Yields: 12 servings

White Chocolate
& Bittersweet Chocolate
 Cake

Bittersweet Chocolate Layer

15 ounces	bittersweet chocolate
½ cup	unsalted butter, cut into chunks
3 tablespoons	instant coffee dissolved in 3 tablespoons water
6	extra-large eggs, separated
¼ teaspoon	cream of tartar
3 tablespoons	sugar

White Chocolate Layer

12 ounces	white chocolate
½ cup plus 1 tablespoon	water
2 cups	heavy cream

For chocolate mousse layer, melt chocolate and butter together. Stir to hasten melting and to smooth mixture. Remove from heat and whisk in the dissolved coffee powder and egg yolks. Set aside.

In a clean dry bowl, beat egg whites and cream of tartar at medium speed until soft peaks form, slowly sprinkle in the sugar, beating at high speed until stiff. Fold egg whites into chocolate until completely incorporated. Using a spatula, scrape the mouse into a 10" spring form pan, being careful to keep the top half of the pan clean. Place in refrigerator.

For white chocolate mousse layer, melt white chocolate and water. Stir to hasten the melting and to smooth the mixture very well. Whip the cream until soft peaks form. Carefully fold cream into melted white chocolate until completely incorporated.

Remove pan from the refrigerator and immediately turn the white mousse on top of chocolate layer. Use metal spatula to level top perfectly with the rim of the pan. Don't manipulate too long because the white mousse will start to set quickly. **Refrigerate for 4 to 6 hours before unmolding.**

Can be made 2 days in advance and refrigerated covered in the pan or frozen up to a month. Can be decorated with dark chocolate shavings.

Yields: 12 servings

Flourless
Chocolate Cake
with
Chocolate Ganache

Cake

10 ounces	bittersweet or semi-sweet chocolate, chopped
1 ¼ cups	unsalted butter, diced
10	extra-large egg yolks
½ cup plus 6 tablespoons	sugar
2 teaspoons	pure vanilla extract
¼ teaspoons	salt
9	extra-large egg whites

Ganache

8 ounces	bittersweet or semi-sweet chocolate, chopped
1 cup	heavy whipping cream
1½ cups	hazelnuts, toasted & coarsely chopped

Preheat oven to 350°F with racks in centre of oven. Butter 10" diameter springform pan with 2 ¾" high sides. Line bottom of pan with parchment paper round.

Place chocolate and 1 ¼ cups butter in medium metal bowl. Set bowl over saucepan of simmering water; stir until mixture is melted and smooth. Remove bowl from over water; cool to lukewarm, about 10 minutes.

Using electric mixer, beat egg yolks and ½ cup sugar in large bowl until very thick and pale yellow in colour, about 5 minutes. Beat in vanilla and salt. Gently fold chocolate mixture into yolk mixture.

Using clean dry beaters, beat egg whites and remaining 6 tablespoons sugar in another large bowl until peaks form. Fold egg whites in 2 additions. Transfer batter to prepared pan.

Bake cake until tester inserted into centre comes out with moist crumbs attached, about 45 minutes. Cake will be puffed and soufflé-like while baking. Cool cake in pan on rack 15 minutes; cake will fall in centre. Run knife around cake sides to loosen; press edge of cake down to make level with centre. Remove pan sides and cool cake completely.

For the ganache, combine chocolate and cream in medium metal bowl. Set bowl over saucepan of simmering water and stir until chocolate is melted and mixture is smooth. Remove bowl from over water; let stand until ganache cools slightly but is still pourable, about 5 minutes.

Place cooled cake on rack set over rimmed baking sheet. Pour ½ cup ganache over top of cake. Using offset spatula, quickly spread ganache over top and sides of cake. Freeze cake 3 minutes. Pour remaining ganache over top of cake. Working quickly but gently and grasping pan bottom and rack together, slightly tilt rack with cake from side to side, allowing ganache to flow evenly over top and down sides of cake; smooth sides with offset spatula. Press hazelnuts onto sides of cake to adhere. Chill cake until ganache is set.

Cake with ganache can be made 1 day ahead. Cover cake with dome and keep refrigerated. Let stand at room temperature 45 minutes before serving.

Yields: 10-12 servings

Fruit *Crisp*

Fruit Filling

3 to 4 cups	your favourite fruit cut into medium sized cubes:
	apples and cinnamon
	blueberry-peach
	mango-peach
	strawberry-rhubarb

Crumble

1 cup	pecans, chopped
¾ cup	all-purpose flour
⅓ cup	brown sugar
⅓ cup	sugar
½ teaspoon	ground cinnamon
½ cup	butter or margarine
	whipped cream or ice cream, for serving

Preheat oven to 375°F and grease 9" oven safe pie or quich style dish. Set aside.

Combine fruit if using more than one and spoon into prepared dish.

Combine pecans, flour, sugars and cinnamon in small bowl. Cut in butter or margarine with pastry blender until mixture is crumbly.

Sprinkle crumble over fruit and bake for 40-45 minutes or until top is golden brown.

Serve with whipped cream or ice cream.

Yields: 6-8 servings

Molten Chocolate Cakes

5 ounces	bittersweet or semi-sweet chocolate, chopped
10 tablespoons	unsalted butter
3	extra-large eggs
3	extra-large egg yolks
1½ cups	icing sugar
½ cups	all-purpose flour
	vanilla ice cream, for serving

Preheat oven to 450°F. Butter six soufflé dishes or custard cups.

Stir chocolate and butter in heavy medium saucepan over low heat until melted. Cool slightly. Whisk eggs and egg yolks in large bowl to blend. Whisk in sugar, then chocolate mixture and flour. Pour batter into dishes, dividing equally.

Bake cakes until sides are set but centre remains soft and runny, about 11 minutes or up to 14 minutes for batter that was refrigerated. Run small knife around cakes to loosen. Immediately turn cakes out onto plates.

Can be made 1 day ahead left in fridge to chill until ready to bake. Serve with ice cream.

Yields: 6 servings

Key *Lime* Pie

Crust

1 cup plus 2 ½ tablespoons	graham cracker crumbs
5 tablespoons	unsalted butter, melted
⅓ cup	sugar

Filling

3	extra-large egg yolks
1 ½ teaspoons	grated zest of 2 limes
1-14 ounce	can sweetened condensed milk
⅔ cup	freshly squeezed lime juice
	whipped cream, for serving

Preheat oven to 350°F. For the graham cracker crust, butter a 9" pie pan.

Add melted butter and sugar to graham crumbs and pulse or stir until combined. Press the mixture into the bottom and sides of the pie pan, forming a neat border around the edge. Bake the crust until set and golden, about 8 minutes. Set aside on a wire rack; leave the oven on.

For the filling, beat the egg yolks and lime zest at high speed until very fluffy, about 5 minutes in an electric mixer with the wire-whisk attachment. Gradually add the condensed milk and continue to beat until thick, 3 or 4 minutes longer. Lower the mixer speed and slowly add the lime juice, mixing just until combined. Do not overmix. Pour the mixture into the crust. Bake for 10 minutes or until the filling has just set. Cool on a wire rack, then refrigerate. Freeze for 15 to 20 minutes before serving. Serve pie very cold.

Top each piece with a dollop of whipped cream.

Yields: 8 servings

Apple Tart

1 sheet	frozen puff pastry, thawed
3 medium	Golden Delicious apples, peeled, cored & very thinly sliced
2 tablespoons	unsalted butter, melted
3 tablespoons	cinnamon sugar (or 3 tablespoons sugar mixed with ½ teaspoon ground cinnamon)
¼ cup	apricot jam, melted

Preheat oven to 400°F. Line baking sheet with parchment paper.

Unfold pastry on parchment paper. Using tines of fork pierce ½" border around edge of pastry then pierce centre all over.

Arrange apples atop pastry in 4 rows, overlapping apple slices and leaving border clear. Brush apples with melted butter; sprinkle with cinnamon sugar.

Bake 30 minutes. Brush melted jam over apples. Bake tart until golden, about 8 minutes longer.

Serve warm or at room temperature.

Yields: 6-8 servings

Roasted *Peach* Streusel

5 tablespoons	unsalted butter, melted & divided
4	ripe but firm peaches, halved & pitted
⅓ cup	slivered almonds, toasted & cooled
⅓ cup	all-purpose flour
⅓ cup	sugar
	whipped cream, for serving

Preheat oven to 425°F with rack in middle position.

Drizzle 2 tablespoons of butter over bottom of 9" baking dish or pie plate and arrange peach halves cut sides up. Pulse almonds, flour, sugar and remaining 3 tablespoons butter in a food processor until clumps form. Top peaches with streusel and bake until peaches are tender and streusel is browned, about 20 minutes (if browning too quickly, loosely cover with foil).

Serve peaches warm with whipped cream.

Yields: 6-8 servings

Michelle's

Banana **Cake**

3	large very ripe bananas
¼ cup	margarine
1 cup	sugar
2	extra-large eggs
1 teaspoon	pure vanilla extract
1 teaspoon	baking soda
1 teaspoon	baking powder
1 cup	whole wheat flour
1 cup	flour
½ cup	fresh orange juice
½ cup	dark chocolate chips

Preheat oven to 350°F. Spray bundt, tube or loaf pan with non-stick spray.

Purée bananas until smooth. Set aside.

Beat margarine, sugar, eggs and vanilla until light, about 3 to 4 minutes. Blend in bananas. Add baking soda and baking powder to flour and add alternately with orange juice. Mix just until blended.

Stir in chocolate chips. Spread evenly in pan or dish. Bake for 45-50 minutes until golden brown.

Can also be baked into 12 muffins.

Yields: 8-10 servings

Bubby
Franni's Butter
Cookies

½ cup	unsalted butter, at room temperature
½ cup	sugar
2 teaspoons	pure vanilla extract
2	extra-large egg yolks
2 cups	all-purpose flour
2 teaspoons	baking powder
1 tablespoon	sour cream

Preheat oven to 325°F and line baking sheet with parchment paper.

Beat butter, sugar and vanilla together until smooth and creamy. Mix in egg yolks until incorporated, scraping down and sides of bowl at least once.

Add baking powder to flour and mix into batter alternately with sour cream, just until incorporated. Scrape onto a floured board and knead a few times, just until dough is smooth.

Dough can be rolled out and cut into shapes or rolled into a log with plastic wrap and refrigerated until firm enough to slice.

Once shapes have been made or log has been sliced, about ⅛" thick, place them on baking sheet about an inch apart.

Bake until just beginning to turn golden around edges, about 16-18 min.

Yields: 2 dozen cookies

Photograph of my daughter, Frankie who is named after my grandmother.

Bubby
Shirley's Chocolate
Cake

Chocolate mixture

4 ounces	semi-sweet chocolate
1 cup	milk
1 teaspoon	pure vanilla extract

Cake

½ cup	(1 stick) unsalted butter
2 cups	sugar
2	extra-large eggs
1 teaspoon	baking soda
3 tablespoons	hot water
2 cups	all-purpose flour
½ cup	milk

Preheat oven to 350°F. Grease 8" round cake pan.

Begin by melting chocolate and milk in microwave or on the stove. When smooth, add 1 teaspoon vanilla and set aside.

For the cake, cream butter and sugar in electric mixer or by hand. Add eggs and incorporate well. Dissolve baking soda in 3 tablespoons hot water and gradually add to batter. Add flour alternately with milk and then add the chocolate mixture. Bake for 1 hour.

Yields: 10-12 servings

One of my grandmother's original type-written recipes.

Chocolate

3 cups	all-purpose flour
⅔ cup	gourmet baking cocoa powder
1 teaspoon	baking soda
1 teaspoon	baking powder
½ teaspoon	salt
1 cup	(2 sticks) unsalted butter, at room temperature
2 cups	sugar
3	extra-large eggs
1 ½ teaspoons	pure vanilla extract
½ cup	semi-sweet chocolate chips
½ cup	white chocolate chips
¼ cup	skor chips
¾ cup	slivered almonds, toasted

Preheat oven to 350°F. Line baking sheet with parchment paper.

Combine flour, cocoa powder, baking soda, baking powder, and salt in large bowl. Beat butter and sugar until smooth. Add eggs and vanilla and blend with butter mixture. Add flour mixture and mix until well combined. Fold in nuts, chocolate chips and skor chips. Divide into 2 or 3 pieces.

Form into logs and space well apart on parchment-lined baking sheet as the dough expands. Bake for 35 minutes. Cool slightly and then slice on angle. Return to oven, **lower heat to 300°F** and bake for another 10 to 15 minutes until firm.

Yields: 2 dozen biscotti

Michelle Little & Autumn Wood

Dried Cranberry & White Chocolate Biscotti

2½ cups	all-purpose flour
1 teaspoon	baking powder
½ teaspoon	salt
1 ½ cups	sugar
½ cup	(1 stick) unsalted butter or margarine, at room temperature
2	extra-large eggs
1 teaspoon	pure almond extract
1½ cups	dried cranberries
1	egg white
6 ounces	white chocolate, chopped, or white chocolate chips

Preheat oven to 350°F. Line heavy large baking sheet with parchment paper.

Combine 2 ½ cups flour, 1 teaspoon baking powder and ½ teaspoon salt in medium bowl; whisk to blend and set aside.

Using electric mixer beat sugar, butter, 2 eggs and almond extract in large bowl until well blended. Mix in flour mixture until combined then add dried cranberries. Divide dough in half. Using floured hands, shape each piece into 2 ½" wide, 9 ½" long, 1" high log.

Transfer both logs to prepared baking sheet, spacing evenly. Whisk egg white in small bowl until foamy; brush egg white glaze on top and sides of each log.

Bake logs until golden brown (logs will spread), about 35 minutes. Cool completely on sheet on rack. Maintain oven temperature. Transfer logs to work surface. Discard parchment. Using serrated knife, cut logs on diagonal into ½" wide slices. Arrange slices, cut side down, on same sheet. Bake 10 minutes; turn biscotti over. Bake until just beginning to colour, about 5 minutes. Transfer biscotti to rack.

Stir white chocolate in top of double boiler over simmering water until smooth. Remove from over water. Using fork, drizzle chocolate over biscotti or dip biscotti on either side in white chocolate. Let stand until chocolate sets, about 30 minutes.

Can be baked 1 week ahead. Freeze in airtight container without white chocolate coating. Thaw to room temperature.

Yields: 28 pieces

Timeless Roly Poly

Dough

3	extra-large eggs
1 cup	sugar
1 cup	vegetable or canola oil
¼ cup	fresh orange juice
3 teaspoons	baking powder
3½ cups	all-purpose flour

Filling

raspberry and/or apricot jam
raisins or dried cranberries
chopped walnuts
ground cinnamon

Preheat oven to 375°F. Put oven rack in middle position and line baking sheet with parchment paper.

For dough, combine all ingredients to make soft dough. Divide into 3 equal parts. Roll out each separately on lightly floured board to ¼" thickness.

Spread jam to within ½" of edges. Add raisins and walnuts covering the jam. Sprinkle with cinnamon. Roll up as a log. Brush with egg wash (1 tablespoon water whisked into 1 extra-large egg) and sprinkle with cinnamon sugar (1 tablespoon sugar mixed with 1 teaspoon cinnamon).

Bake for 30 minutes. Cool. Cut into slices.

Yields: 24-30 slices

Mom's
Rugelach

Dough

½ cup	(1 stick) unsalted butter, cut into bits
4 ounces	cold cream cheese, cut into bits
1 cup	all-purpose flour
½ teaspoon	salt

Filling

⅔ cup	walnuts, finely chopped
⅓ cup	sugar
1 teaspoon	ground cinnamon
	raspberry jam
	milk

Preheat oven to 350°F. Put oven rack in middle position and line baking sheet with parchment paper.

Whisk together flour and salt in a bowl. Beat together butter and cream cheese in large bowl with electric mixer until combined well. Add flour mixture and stir with wooden spoon until soft dough forms. Gather dough into a ball and wrap in plastic wrap, then flatten (in wrap) into a roughly 7" x 5" rectangle. Chill until firm.

Cut dough into 2 pieces and roll out each piece into a 12" x 8" rectangle on a well-floured surface with a floured rolling pin. Transfer dough to a sheet of parchment. Alternatively, you may roll each piece into a circle and cut each into 12 equal triangles.

Lightly pulse the walnuts, sugar and cinnamon in a chopper and set aside. Arrange each dough rectangle on work surface with long side nearest you. Spread enough jam evenly over dough with offset spatula leaving a small amount of dough visible all around. Sprinkle walnut-sugar mixture thinly covering preserves, leaving some mixture for topping.

Using parchment as an aid, roll up dough tightly into log. Place seam side down, in lined baking sheet, then pinch ends closed and tuck underneath. Repeat with second piece of rolled dough. Cut each roll crosswise at 1" intervals. If dough is too soft to cut, chill until firmer, 20 to 30 minutes. Gently brush each piece with milk and sprinkle with remaining topping.

Bake until golden, 45 to 50 minutes. Cool completely before removing from baking sheet, about 30 minutes.

Yields: 2 dozen pieces

Soft & Chewy
Oatmeal **Raisin** Cookies

1 cup	(2 sticks) unsalted butter, at room temperature
1 cup	brown sugar
¼ cup	sugar
2	extra-large eggs
1 tablespoon	pure vanilla extract
1 tablespoon	molasses
1½ cups	all-purpose flour
1 teaspoon	baking soda
1½ teaspoons	ground cinnamon
½ teaspoon	salt
3 cups	old-fashioned rolled oats
1 cup	raisins
½ cup	walnuts, toasted & chopped (optional)

Preheat oven to 350°F and line two large baking sheets with parchment paper.

Using hand mixer or stand mixer fitted with paddle attachment, cream softened butter and both sugars together on medium speed until smooth, about 2 minutes. Add eggs and mix on high until combined, about 1 minute. Scrape down the sides and bottom of the bowl as needed. Add vanilla and molasses and mix on high until combined. Set aside.

In separate bowl, toss flour, baking soda, cinnamon, and salt together. Slowly incorporate into batter and mix on low speed until combined. Beat in oats, raisins, and walnuts (if desired) on low speed.

Dough will be thick and very sticky. **Chill the dough for an hour in refrigerator.**

Roll balls of dough, about 2 tablespoons of dough per cookie and place 2 inches apart on baking sheets. Bake for 11-13 minutes until very lightly browned on the sides. The centres will look very soft and undone. Remove from oven and let cool on baking sheet for 5 minutes before transferring to wire rack to cool completely. The cookies will continue to set on the baking sheet during this time.

If chilling for longer, (up to 2 days) allow to sit at room temperature for at least 30 minutes before rolling and baking.

Yields: 2 dozen cookies

Jewish Traditions

Halishkes Cabbage Rolls

3	large curly cabbage
2 pounds	minced beef
2	sweet onions, finely diced
1 cup	white rice
2 ½ teaspoons	salt
½ teaspoon	pepper
3-28 ounce	canned diced tomatoes
1 large	bottle Heinz chili sauce
1 ½ cups	brown sugar
1 teaspoon	fresh lemon juice

Cook cabbage in boiling water for a few minutes just until outer leaves pull away easily from head. From the 3 cabbages, set aside 24 large leaves for rolls. In a small bowl, combine the beef, onion, rice, salt and pepper; mix well. When leaves are cool enough to handle, use a paring knife to cut away the thick centre stem from each leaf, without cutting all the way through.

Place about ¼ cup meat mixture on a cabbage leaf; overlap cut ends of leaf. Fold in sides. Beginning from the cut end, roll up tightly. Repeat until all leaves are used and set aside.

Combine tomatoes, chili sauce, sugar and lemon juice in large pot and bring to simmer to blend flavours. Slice the leftover cabbage and place on bottom of roasting pan large enough to hold cabbage rolls snuggly without overlapping. Pour enough sauce over the cabbage to lightly coat. Arrange the cabbage rolls seam side down over sauce and then pour remaining sauce on top. Cover and bake at 350° for 1½-2 hours or until cabbage rolls are tender.

You can add raisins to the filling if desired. Great for Sukkot. Freezes well.

Yields: 24 rolls

Chicken Liver Pâté

3	extra-large eggs
1 pound	fresh chicken livers
2	medium sweet onions
1	small sweet onion
4	garlic cloves
3 tablespoons	extra-virgin olive oil
2 tablespoons	medium-dry sherry or brandy
1 teaspoon	sugar
	salt & pepper

Hard-boil eggs and cool. Peel eggs and chill covered until ready to use.

Trim chicken livers and pat dry between paper towels. Chop medium onions and garlic. In a large heavy skillet, cook chopped onions and garlic in olive oil over moderate heat, stirring, until golden, about 10 minutes.

Increase heat to medium high and add chicken livers. Cook mixture, stirring occasionally, until livers are cooked through but still barely pink inside, 5 to 8 minutes. Transfer mixture to a bowl and cool. Finely chop enough of small onion to measure ⅓ cup and in a food processor pulse together with 2 hard-boiled eggs until well blended. Add liver mixture, sherry or brandy, sugar, and salt and pepper to taste and blend until smooth.

Transfer pâté to a small serving bowl and cool. Chill pâté, covered, at least **4 hours and up to 2 days.** Just before serving, separate yolk and white from remaining hard-boiled egg and force them separately through a coarse sieve onto pâté.

Serve pâté with toasts or crackers.

Yields: 4-6 servings

Best Ever

Half Recipe

7 ½ cups	bread flour
¾ cup	sugar
1 tablespoon	salt
2	extra-large eggs
½ cup	canola oil
3 teaspoons	bread machine yeast
2 cups	lukewarm water

Full Recipe

14-15 cups	bread flour
1 ½ cups	sugar
2 tablespoons	salt
4	extra-large eggs
1 cup	canola oil
6 teaspoons	bread machine yeast
1 tablespoon	sugar
4 cups	lukewarm water

Place all ingredients in bread maker. Once bread maker is complete, shape as desired.

Prepare egg wash by whisking 1 egg with 1 tablespoon water. With pastry brush, glaze challah on top and all around with egg wash. Sprinkle with desired toppings.

Cover gently and let rise 30 minutes more in warm place. Preheat oven to 350°F convection. Bake for 35-45 minutes.

Our favourite toppings include rosemary and coarse sea salt, classic sesame seeds and a sweet topping.

Yields: Half recipe makes 2 challahs. Full recipe makes 4 challahs.

Michelle Little & Autumn Wood

Bubby *Ida's* **Matzah** Balls

1 cup   water
½ cup   vegetable or canola oil
1 cup   matzah meal
3   extra-large eggs
         salt

Bring large pot of lightly salted water to a boil. In another pot, bring 1 cup of water and the oil to boil. Remove from the heat and add the matzah meal all at once, stirring until incorporated and pulls away from the sides of the pot, cool. Add eggs, one at time, stirring until combined. Add salt to taste.

Keeping hands wet, form into balls and gently add to the boiling water. Bring temperature to simmer and cook until fluffy and rise to top of pot, approximately 20 minutes. Gently remove from water.

Add to chicken soup recipe for the full experience! Recipe can easily be doubled or tripled for a large crowd.

Yields: 12 matzah balls

Bubby *Shirley's* **Honey** Cake

3	extra-large eggs
½ cup	sugar
½ cup	vegetable or canola oil
¾ cup	honey
2 ¼ cups	all-purpose flour
1 ½ teaspoons	baking powder
¾ teaspoon	allspice
¾ cup	strong tea
¾ teaspoon	baking soda
¾ cup	walnuts, halved

Preheat oven to 350°F. Grease ring pan.

Dissolve baking soda in tea and set aside. Whisk eggs, sugar, oil, and honey. Add dry ingredients alternately with tea mixture. Fold in walnuts.

Bake for 50-60 minutes.

Yields: 12 servings

Saturday
Cholent

4 cups	packaged "cholent mix"
6	onions, peeled & thinly sliced
6 pounds	flanken, cut into large cubes
	salt & pepper
1 teaspoon	paprika
2	garlic cloves, minced
5 pounds	potatoes, peeled & quartered
⅔ cup	barley

Preheat oven to 200°F.

Wash beans from cholent mix very well. Brown onions in a little bit of oil, in skillet.

Rub meat generously with seasonings and garlic. Place all ingredients into large oven-proof pot with a tightly fitting lid.

Add boiling water to cover and season generously with salt and pepper. Cover the pot very tightly. Place in oven for **minimum 12 hours or preferably overnight.**

Yields: 8-10 servings

Homemade *Gefilte* Fish

For water (per pot)

Two pots are preferred when making 9 pounds of fish

25 cups	water
2 medium	vidalia onions, cut up
2 pounds	carrots, cut on diagonal
3 cups	sugar
	salt & pepper

For fish

9 pounds	minced white fish
4	large sweet onions; finely minced until watery
9	extra-large eggs
1 cup	matzah meal
4 ½ cups	sugar
4 teaspoons	salt
	horseradish, for serving

For the water, bring all ingredients to light boil. As soon as heated, simmer.

For the fish, place minced fish in large mixing bowl. Add minced onion and eggs and combine well. Add sugar and salt. Add matzah meal and mix until mixture is still quite loose, but seems able to form into balls. Let stand 5 minutes then form into medium oval sized balls and gently place in simmering water.

Loosely cover and cook for 1 ½ to 2 hours. Do not allow to boil. Leave in pot until cool. Transfer to container, placing carrots on top. Reserve fish sauce (or "yoach") for serving.

Recipe can easily be halved; use one pot of water. Serve with horseradish for best flavour.

Yields: 36 large fish balls

Holiday
Hamantashen

Dough

4	extra-large eggs, lightly beaten
1 cup	vegetable oil
1 cup	sugar
4 teaspoons	baking powder
½ teaspoon	salt
(approx.) 5 to 6 cups	all-purpose flour
½ cup	fresh orange juice

Filling

1 pound	prunes, pitted
½ cup	raisins
½ cup	dates
½ cup	walnuts
¼ cup	sugar
1 teaspoon	ground cinnamon
2 teaspoons	fresh orange juice

Preheat oven to 350°F. Line baking sheets with parchment paper.

Process prunes, raisins and dates until coarsely ground, about 12 to 15 seconds. Add the walnuts and process with 3 or 4 quick on/offs, until finely chopped. Add sugar, cinnamon and orange juice and process just until combined adding more orange juice if necessary. Set aside.

In electric mixer, beat eggs and oil together until pale coloured. Gradually add the sugar, baking powder, salt and the flour alternately with orange juice. Mix on low speed to combine, scraping down the sides of the bowl with a rubber spatula. Gradually add the last cup of flour, making soft dough, which is not sticky. If necessary, add a little extra flour. Divide the dough into 4 sections and roll out each piece as thinly as possible on a well-floured surface into a large rectangle. Cut out circles using a cookie cutter or the rim of a drinking glass. Place a tablespoon of filling in the centre of the circle and pinch edges firmly together to create a triangle. Glaze each hamantashen with thin layer of 1 beaten egg with pastry brush.

Bake for 20 minutes, until golden brown.

Yields: 24-30

Pickled
Salmon

Salmon

2 pounds	salmon filet; boneless & skinless cut into 1-1 ½" wide pieces

Brine

1 cup	water
½ cup	sugar
1 cup	vinegar
½ cup	ketchup
	salt
2	handfuls of pickling spices
2	sweet onions, thinly sliced

To poach salmon, estimate the amount of water you'll need to just cover the salmon pieces. Bring the water to a boil and then reduce to a simmer. Add the salmon pieces and cover until opaque; approximately 5-7 minutes. Make sure the liquid remains at a gentle simmer and does not boil. Gently remove salmon with a slotted spoon.

To make the brine, boil water in another pot and add ½ cup sugar until is dissolves. Cool and then add remaining ingredients except the onions.

Place a layer of salmon in large glass dish and scatter onions underneath and in between slices of fish to distribute flavour. Once you have finished this, pour the well cooled brine over the top of the fish covering completely and **marinate for minimum 2-3 days.**

Yields: 4-6 servings

My beautiful family
Izzy, Josh, Benji, (me) & Frankie

Brunch

Family Favourite
Cheese **Pie**

Crust and Topping

2 cups	cornflakes, crushed
1 ½ cups	all-purpose flour
½ teaspoon	baking soda
½ cup	(1 stick) unsalted butter, melted
1 cup	brown sugar, packed

Filling

4	extra-large eggs
1 cup	sugar
2 pounds	cottage cheese (bulk)
1 cup	sour cream
1 teaspoon	pure vanilla extract
2 tablespoons	all-purpose flour
1	lemon, grated rind

Preheat oven to 325°F.

For the crust, mix ingredients well and set aside 1 ½ cups for topping.

Combine filling ingredients. Pat all but reserved 1 ½ cups of topping on bottom of 9" x 13" baking dish.

Pour batter onto crust. Cover filling with the topping. Bake for 1 hour.

Cheese pie is delicious with plain yogurt or sour cream.

Yields: 10 servings

Easy Blender
Hollandaise Sauce

3	extra-large egg yolks
1 tablespoon	fresh lemon juice
½ teaspoon	salt
⅛ teaspoon	cayenne (optional)
10 tablespoons	unsalted butter

Melt butter slowly in a small pot. Try not to let it boil; you want the moisture in the butter to remain there and not steam away. Add the egg yolks, lemon juice, salt and cayenne (if desired) into blender. Blend the egg yolk mixture at a medium to medium-high speed until it lightens in colour, about 20-30 seconds.

Once the yolks have lightened in colour, drizzle in the hot melted butter slowly, while the blender is going. Continue to blend for another couple seconds after the butter is incorporated. Turn off the blender and taste the sauce.

It should be buttery, lemony and just lightly salty. If it is not salty or lemony enough, you can add a little lemon juice or salt to taste. If you want a thinner consistency, add a little warm water. Pulse briefly to incorporate the ingredients one more time. Store until needed in a warm spot, like on or next to the stovetop. Use within an hour or so on top of poached eggs.

Yields: 4 servings

Homemade *Monkey* Bread

Dough

2 ¼ teaspoons	(1 package) instant yeast
¼ cup	warm water
¼ cup	warm milk
⅓ cup	unsalted butter, melted
¼ cup	sugar
2	extra-large eggs
1 teaspoon	salt
5 cups	all-purpose flour

Coating

¾ cup	unsalted butter
1 ¼ cups	sugar
1 tablespoon	ground cinnamon
⅔ cup	brown sugar
1 teaspoon	pure vanilla extract

Glaze

1 cup	icing sugar
3 tablespoons	heavy cream
½ teaspoon	pure vanilla extract

Monkey bread tastes best served on the same day, but will stay fresh for 3 days if stored covered at room temperature or in the refrigerator.

Begin by making dough. In large mixing bowl, dissolve yeast in warm water. Stir it around a bit and let it sit for about 2 minutes. Add milk, melted butter, sugar, eggs, salt and 3 cups of flour. Beat on high speed for 3 minutes (using a dough hook if you have a stand mixer or using a hand mixer). By hand, add enough remaining flour to form a firm dough, about 5 cups total.

Turn the dough onto a floured surface. Knead until smooth and elastic, about 5 minutes. Do not over-knead. This will yield a tough, chewy bread. The dough is ready when it is smooth and when you can poke it with a finger and it springs back. Form dough into a smooth ball and place into a large greased bowl, turning once to grease the top. Cover tightly with plastic wrap or aluminum foil and **refrigerate for 8 hours or overnight**.

Preheat oven to 350°F. Spray 10-12 cup bundt pan with cooking spray.

For the coating, melt ½ cup of butter in small bowl. Mix sugar and cinnamon together in another small bowl. Set aside.

Punch the cold dough down very gently to allow the air bubbles to release. Pull apart pieces and roll into balls, about 1¼" in diameter. You will need 40-45 balls total, so be modest with size. Dip each ball, one by one into melted butter and then generously roll in the cinnamon-sugar mixture to coat them. You may need more cinnamon-sugar depending how heavy you coat each ball. Arrange them in the bundt pan as you go.

Melt the remaining ¼ cup of butter and whisk in the brown sugar and vanilla until combined. Pour the buttery mixture over the dough balls in the bundt pan. Bake for 30-35 minutes or until golden brown on top. Cover loosely with foil if the top browns too quickly. Cool for 5-10 minutes and invert onto a large serving plate.

Simply whisk all of the glaze ingredients together and pour over the bread. You may either cut the bread into generous slices or let everyone pick off the gooey pieces themselves.

Yields: 10-12 servings

Overnight Baked *French Toast* with **Blueberries**

1 cup	brown sugar
1 ½ teaspoons	ground cinnamon
¼ cup	(½ stick) unsalted butter, melted
12 slices	challah
1 ½ cups	fresh blueberries
5	extra-large eggs
1 ½ cups	milk
1 teaspoon	pure vanilla extract
½ teaspoon	salt
	pure maple syrup, for serving

Preheat oven to 350°F .

Combine brown sugar, cinnamon and melted butter. Mix well. Sprinkle ⅓ of mixture evenly in bottom of 9" x 13" pan. Cover with 6 slices of bread; you may have to cut pieces to fill pan. Sprinkle another ⅓ of mixture over bread and scatter berries on top. Place remaining bread on fruit. Sprinkle with remaining sugar mixture.

Beat eggs, milk and vanilla and salt together. Pour evenly over bread. Press down lightly. Cover with plastic wrap and **refrigerate overnight**. Bake uncovered for 40-45 minutes until puffed and golden.

For added sweetness and decadence, serve with pure maple syrup.

Yields: 12 servings

Bubby Shirley's

Blueberry
Muffins

½ cup	(1 stick) unsalted butter, at room temperature
2	extra-large eggs
1 cup	sugar
½ cup	milk
2 cups	all-purpose flour
2 teaspoons	baking powder
2 cups	fresh blueberries

Preheat oven to 400°F.

Dust blueberries with a little flour and sugar and set aside.

Soften butter and add eggs, one at a time. Add sugar and mix until incorporated. Add baking powder to flour and add alternately to batter with milk. When the batter is fully combined, gently fold in berries. Pour batter into muffins cups and bake for 20-25 minutes.

Yields: 12 muffins

Index

Acknowledgments

First and foremost, I must thank my mom. **Mom**, without you, this cookbook would not exist. Every recipe is yours; your ingredients, your love, your dedication. Thank you for providing me with the makings needed to fulfill my dreams. I love you.

Julie Siciliano and **Sabrina Campanelli**, I knew you were both a perfect fit for this cookbook from the moment we first met. Thank you for your patience and talent. You made this process so easy and I was always comforted knowing I can trust you.

To a visionary photographer, **Ariel Tarr**, your photographs make every dish come to life. I could not have imagined better photographs for this cookbook. Thank you!

Michelle Diamond, you work magic! Your skills and techniques are highlighted in this cookbook. Thank you for all your notes during the process and for helping capture the true taste and flavour of our recipes.

Michelle Little and **Autumn Wood**, thank you for the beautiful additions we were lucky enough to feature in this cookbook. You are both so very talented and I look forward to working with you in the future.

Thank you to the ever-talented hairdresser and stylist, **Rima Nasr** and my favourite makeup artist of all time, **Jessica Cohen** for beautifying my mom and I for the photographs. You always make us feel and look so glamorous!

To my cousin, **Alecsandra Kakon**, thank you for your time in helping me edit this cookbook and for all your advice. I'm happy we had time to spend together!

To my best friends, **Cassie and Brian**, I know I can always count on you to eat my food, but most importantly, I know I can count on you for anything at all.

All my **gal pals**, you know who you are! I'm always in awe of your accomplishments and constant support for one another. Thank you for always cheering me on. You girls make life so fun and exciting. Keep being awesome!

I thank G-d for the biggest family I am blessed to be a part of. **Jack, Pascale, Gabriella, Daniella and Erica, Avi, Nancy, Jonah and Ethan, Sari, Albert, Olivia, Alex, Romy and Maya and Rochelle and Jeffrey,** family meals and spending time together is always something I look forward to. You're all talented chefs and I'm proud to share my culinary adventures with you all. Thank you for your constant love and support.

Bubby Shirley, thank you for your contribution to this cookbook. Your timeless and delicious recipes will always be a staple in my home and in my heart.

In loving memory of my dearly missed and remembered, **Bubby Franni** and my great-grandmother, **Bubby Ida** whose recipes and inspiration provided some of these cherished recipes.

Mom, Dad, Warren, Ashley, Max, Dylan and Adam, thanks for always believing in me and supporting my wishes and dreams. Everything is possible with you. I love you.

To the love of my life and best friend, **Josh**. Thank you for pushing me to believe in myself and for always encouraging me to fulfill whatever desire I have in life. You've always been my biggest fan in the kitchen. While I cook and bake a lot for you in our kitchen, I think our greatest recipes are our beautiful children. **Benji, Frankie and Izzy**, you complete our life. I love you, even if you only want to eat rice cakes for dinner.

Last but definitely not least, thank you to the higher power, **HaShem**. Thank you for blessing me with the energy and passion to achieve something special with my Mom. This experience is something I will always cherish. I hope to use the success of this cookbook for good and to help others less fortunate.

Produced by
Randi Cola & Michelle Cola Hasen

Photography | Prop Styling
Ariel Tarr
www.arieltarr.com

Food Styling
Michelle Diamond

Additional Photography
Michelle Little & Autumn Wood

Props
Looks Like White, Crate and Barrel Canada, Atelier Make

Graphic Design
Julie Siciliano & Sabrina Campanelli, Cassi Design
www.cassidesign.com

Printed in Canada
TC Transcontinental Printing

ISBN: 978-1-9990986-0-5

Like Mother Like Daughter cookbook includes some traditional, some new and some borrowed recipes that hold a special place in my heart. Please understand that errors may appear. The recipes produced may vary, due to the quality of ingredients and of course, the love and time taken by each individual chef.